LISTEN
WITH
YOUR
HEART

ALVINA Y. PLATT-GREGORY

Ordering Information:

BookTrail Agency
8838 Sleepy Hollow Rd.
Kansas City, MO 64114

Printed in the United States of America

Contents

I dedicate this book to the Holy Trinity: God, Jesus and the Holy Spirit. Thank you for giving me the courage to obey and put it into print for others to listen with their hearts as they read each poem that will speak to them right where they are.

My Speaking Heart

I dedicate my life to the Holy Trinity.

Whom I love, honor and respect forever throughout eternity.

Thank you for compassion to reach the mark,

The passion to live and do my part.

The courage to stop complaining and start,

Listening… to my speaking heart.

Thank You!

An Affirmation

I am a representative of God. I won't think more highly of myself than I ought.

I will keep God's statues and commandments and please Him, because of this He will not put the diseases of the Egyptians on me for he is the Lord thy God that healeth thee (me).

Become

Jesus said become like me for I became like you
To experience all the things that you will go through.

Meditate on My Word, it's for your making
Learn to give to others instead of taking.

My love for you goes beyond all measures
My mercy and grace are my greatest treasures
For you to receive, embrace and be blessed
To rejoice and praise me with your very best.
The best that you can be, in all that you do
Give your best to all, not just a chosen few!

I love you and if you love me
You will do all these things to the best of your ability.

BECOME LIKE ME!

God's Best

God called you to be your best
Don't murmur or complain when faced with a test.
Stand firm against the perils of time and listen
 To God proclaim that you are mine.

You can tell by the manner in which you carry yourself
If you are walking in His image or
As someone else.

The glow on your face reflects His grace
With strategies for perfection, you set your pace
To cross the finish line and come in first place!
Then God said with His chest held high,
You are my best, come forth and draw nigh.

Alvina Y. Platt-Gregory

Choose Life and Live

A new day is here and time is running out…
Consider your ways and lift the Lord in praise,
You know not the moment, the minutes or days left!

To go forth and reach and teach and preach,
To the lost, lifeless, dumbfounded sheep.

Doing His will is really a thrill,
It is exciting, adventurous complete with goose bumps and chills.
No heavy burdens to hold you down,
When God speaks, it is in surround sound!
Wherever you go, you will hear the echo
So share it with others so they can know,
How sweet it is to live for Him,
Stop drowning in life and learn how to swim!

Perfect fitness for the heart, mind, body and soul
Let the healing begin, step back and behold…
The beauty of the Lord, His mercy and grace
Keeping His commandments will help you run this race,
With patience, kindness, meekness and love
That is all that is required from our creator above.
Jesus said I am this dark worlds' light.
Stop walking in darkness, today, this season,
Why dont you choose life!

Born Again

Heavenly Father, I come before you with an open heart, to thank you for dying for my sins.

I believe you died, arose, so that I might be born again.

I believe you died so that I might live and you might live in me.

Thank you Jesus for loving me and making me free,

So that I may have a place with thee in all eternity.

In Jesus name, I pray, in His word I will stay. AMEN!

Born To Die

Blessed are those who mourn
The death of those who are born,
Their destiny is to die.

The life he lives, is the life he has to give
To God in truth not living a lie.
Before that day, come what may, giving all to God.
He did his best; he passed the test, rarely stopping to take a rest.

Thank you Lord for peace of mind and a spirit that is oh so kind.
We are born to die, a known fact on earth,
Die only in the natural if we receive the spiritual birth.

Beware!

Beware of the stranger… he might take advantage of you.

Beware of those friends that might try too.

Beware of the hell raiser…or you may die.

Beware of the peacemakers…some of them lie.

Beware of all the people in this unstable world.

BEWARE!

Trust in Jesus, not in man

Seek His face and not His hand.

There is a thin line between love and hate

Examine yourself before it is too late.

BEWARE!

Alvina Y. Platt-Gregory

3 G's To Live By

Go…forth and do not stop until the Lord bids you to stop.
Grow…in the knowledge and admiration of the Lord.
Glow…with the indwelling of the Holy Spirit.
Flow…in His presence!

GO, GROW AND GLOW!
Do not stop until you know
The who, what and where
That comes with many stares.

Work diligently to go, grow and glow.
It is not until these three are ago, that in the word of God you will flow,
Since the one who really cares, you will know!

G-12 *

G-12 can keep you from hell
By enforcing the commandments of Jesus,
Do tell…
To love the Lord with all your heart and love your neighbor as a part…
Of yourself as you walk with them to Spiritual Health
Then teach them how to gain the spiritual wealth.
Yes, G-12 can keep you from hell
Not only you but others as well!
*G-12 is the Government of twelve. This is how Jesus taught His disciples.

Alvina Y. Platt-Gregory

Fight!

Fight the good fight of faith every day!

God is your protection, come what may
When you fight the good fight of faith every day.
Fight and subdue because God cares for you.
Stay strong and maintain yourself for God will do everything else.
So fight the good fight of faith every day!

Jesus, I Want You!

I want you Lord! You are the way!
I want you Lord so I will not stray.
 I want you Lord in my life today...
JESUS, I WANT YOU!

I want you Lord, in you I have my being,
I want you Lord, you give life real meaning.
I want you Lord, I am pleading!
JESUS, I WANT YOU!

Dwell in me Lord. I will make this a sacred place,
Dwell in me Lord. I will wear you on my face,
Dwell in me Lord and fill me with your grace!
JESUS, I WANT YOU!

Alvina Y. Platt-Gregory

I Will Remember...

(insert name) must have lived a remarkable life,
 I say this because for many years you were his wife.
He had a great spirit, full of spunk and vim, and
 That is how I will always remember him.

God bless you!

Let

God is in control of all and Jesus is the only way,

He will catch you when you fall and bring you back if you stray!

Let Him shape and mold you as you sit on the Potter's wheel,

Fret not thyself, lean not on your own understanding, stand tall in His word and be still.

Life situations may slap you in the face, turn the other cheek and stay in your place.

Do not try to out run Jesus' pace!

He is your strength and shield,

You are His creation so do the Father's will.

Bend with flexibility, walk and not faint,

You can do all things in Christ, in Him you are a Saint.

The day may be over but life will go on

Drop the weight of being frustrated and LET bygones be bygones!

God Will

When you have done your best, your soul can rest.

You did everything you could, perhaps more than you should.

God will speak peace to your spirit, mind, body and soul.

The destiny of your love one is now in God's hands,

His living was not in vain he was a part of God's plans.

So celebrate his life and remember.

Give Me Rest

Rest now said the body to the mind. Please sit down and give me some rest. I am tired of the stress.

I need to re-coup and re-group to be my best.

Are you putting me through some kind of test?

Do you want to see how far you can go before I sit you down and take over?

Rest now before I knock you down and take what I need, proper rest and nutrition is what it will take to succeed, so give me rest, I need rest!

A little bit of rest, a good night sleep will do and I will forgive you for the things you have put me through, so give me rest…I need rest.

Moving at this pace, sickness is bound to take its toll and I will be too weak to take control.

REST, give me rest and I will give you my best!

Alvina Y. Platt-Gregory

Life In a Funnel

One day my life went from living large and wide to small and narrowing like a funnel.

What happen? What caused the change? What did I do? What did I rearrange?

I sat and though, meditated for a while, retraced my steps from inch to mile.

The bills were overwhelming, like a cloud covering the sun,

Every time the phone would ring, the coward in me wanted to run.

I was snatched from the edge by the stronger one within and pulled it together,

We could not let the weaker me win!

The Holy Spirit brought back to my remembrance, these familiar words swelled in my throat,

Greater is He that is within me, powerful words an Apostle wrote.

I laughed and smiled and danced for a while, snickering over life's little joke.

I am moving towards the light at the end of the tunnel, no longer will I live my life in a funnel.

Life Is A Play

You are not in this world to live for yourself. You are here to help someone else.

You must stop and pray, listen and obey to what God has to say.

He is the creator with the master plan, stop being a hater and be a fan, so you may become a better human.

You live to give and are bless to be a blessing so listen with your heart and learn the part you are to perform daily in this play called life.

Your performance is paving your way to receive applause not heard in the earth but on judgement day for your role in "Accepting the New Birth"!

You are an actor in the play called life so perform with the grace and favor of God,

You were born to play the part and now is the time to start!

Mind Your Mind

There are three parts to the mind: the conscious, the subconscious and the conscience.

Know your mind and then you will have no problems hearing from God above and accepting His unconditional love.

He tells us to transform our minds and think on things that are pure, lovely and kind.

You shall receive the promise for your life after you patiently endure and have experienced the Divine learning process with a guaranteed cure.

Feed your mind with the word of God and get on the right path because an ungodly life just will not last!

No Room To Stray

When you walk by faith and not by sight, God will show you His marvelous light and draw you closer day by day, a guaranteed safe walk with no room to stray.

Excellent With You (God)

I am excellent in all I do. I have an excellent spirit through and through that strengthens my walk and talk with you. In Jesus' Name, there is nothing I cannot do!

Dancing With The Wind

I woke up early this morning

To the sound of a half crushed soda can dancing down the street with the mighty wind.

Whoosh, clickity clank, clickity clank...

 Whoosh, clickity clank, clickity clank...

They danced until the can took a rest in someone's front yard.

Whooooooooooooooooooooooooooooooosh...!

The wind is now looking for a new dance partner.

A Holiday Union

This holiday season, we celebrate something that is greater than great!

The birth of our Lord and Savior, Jesus Christ, and the union of this man and wife.

What a time, what a time this must be, you are going to be a family.

Overwhelmed by two births, no make that three...

Jesus Christ, you and your wife to be.

Don't Wait

It is good to see you all again, a few enemies as well as my friends.

In life, you need the two, one to criticize and the other to encourage you.

Look around at each other and take a deep breath.

Thank the Lord He did not call you home to rest!

There is work to do and many areas have not been touched.

A single few plus one less the majority can accomplish much.

Take my hand and make a stand, let us conquer the problems in our promised land.

The land is those unfinished things in your life, those things you started and tried to

Accomplish without seeking professional advice.

Your land is the fear that is deep inside and holding you back because you don't let God abide!

The upkeep of your land is in your hands, you have the power just know that you can.

Speak to it and put your words into action, it will take confidence and strength to carry on,

This will become a habit before too long.

Go forth until God bids you to stop, you reap what you sow, so sow a bountiful crop!

Don't Think

If you read the word, you will not think it absurd for you be to call by God.

You will find it an honor to be consider to carry out an assignment that seem odd.

Reading the word will speak to you, council and guide you all the way.

Plant the word in your heart, it is the light in the dark and remember to

Speak it every day!

Marital Bliss

Does marital bliss exist? It does if God is in the midst.

In everything you do and in everything you say

He wants to be included in every part of your day!

Do not shut Him out, let Him come in and you will find Him to be an awesome friend.

What God has put together, let no man put asunder!

Keep God in your marriage, so it will not go under!

"Holy" Matrimony

Fatherhood speaks:

The Lord said it is not good for man to be alone, so He made woman, flesh of my flesh and bone of my bone. He made a she from within me and together we will be

Complete in Him, the head of all power and principality.

Motherhood speaks:

I salute you the male side of me, to your spirit, your mind and yes your body.

Nothing can stop us when we touch and agree, what strength and power in this ministry.

I salute you, the male side of me.

Then the Preacher said:

I now pronounce you husband and wife, stay true to your vows this is your partner for life!

Mother's Day

Mother's Day comes in May

At least that is when we celebrate it.

This comes from the heart, what a great place to start in telling you it is underrated.

The mother in you, so proud and true, gives Mother's Day a whole new meaning.

Some of your children have gone on and some you are yet, still weaning.

To face life challenges and handle all we can bare,

When life becomes too much you always have advice to share.

Your heart of gold truly unfolds the mysteries of Motherhood.

You watch and pray for them every day with a spiritual nurturing that is understood.

Admiration follows all you do and say.

 To honor you it is perfectly clear will take more than just one day!

Yes, in all you do, we acknowledge you and your tender loving care.

We thank you for your wisdom and always being there.

HAPPY MOTHER'S DAY!

Alvina Y. Platt-Gregory

Poor Little Fifth Grader

Poor little fifth grader, don't know what to do.

Always so trouble and always so blue.

I cannot do my work, I do not understand,

I do not want to listen to that woman or that man

I want what I want, I do not care who I taunt,

I want what I want, let me have it my way and deal with you another day!

Education is valuable,

I heard them say, the higher the education, the higher the pay.

That is deep, that is dope, hip, hip, hooray!

But, between you and me, I cannot deal with that today.

The New One

Congratulation on the birth of your new one, before you know it, he will be learning how to run and you will be chasing him to- and- fro but that is how the early years are design to go.

Enjoy them because it will not last long, before you know it, he will be big and strong.

It is up to you to train that child and teach him how to wear a smile!

The Face of Age

What does it look like?

Does it look like a child riding his bike or a teen flying a kite?

Does it look like a man who has no insight of does it look like a woman who knows she is right!

The face of age, is it innocent and pure or having a pimple and finding a cure?

Is it weary and stressed because you are not sure, or is it making the right decision because you are mature?

Age is a number counting your existence on earth.

Beginning the count from the day of your birth.

Age is a number you do not have to wear on your face if you have a good attitude, confidence and good taste!

November 29th

November 29th is a wonderful day, it all happened many years ago,

My first son came into the world and since then my heart has been a glow!

November 29th is a wonderful day. This is when my son came to earth to stay.

In my life came so much joy, all because of this baby boy.

My sweet little baby… I felt such love when I called his name

He warmed my heart from the very start with a personality that said he had "game"!

God's gift to me, a lovely spirit so free, he will make his mark and fulfill his destiny.

Keep your head to the sky, any questions, ask God why and be ready to receive His Answer without dispute make sure it is from God, all other voices you rebuke!

Other voices will lead you down a path that might seem right but the end leads to death.

When and if this happens, call the great name of Jesus and say it all in one breath…

JESUS!

Oh Lord

If thou will bless me oh Lord with the wisdom, to share with those who have schisms

How to overcome self-doubt and speak with confidence without a shout.

I pray, you give them a taste of the truth so they can find,

Your joy and have peace of mind.

O Lord I pray that you grant it this day.

A Closer Look

Happy Birthday to you, another year you made it through, escaping many heartaches and pains that come with success and monetary gain.

The dying of a loved one, thank God it was only one, stirred a new life in you.

You returned to your writings, expressing your thoughts and feelings that made you blue.

When you sit and reflect, the year was not so bad, considering the circumstances, it was the best you ever had. The best because of the knowledge you gleaned and the lessons you learned from others treating you mean.

This triggered a closer look at those you call "friend".

Do they really love and care about you or is it all just pretend?

Pastors From God

The Lord is my Shepherd. He sent me to thee, to be fed, nourished and fill the void in me.

You represent His presence, His mercy and grace.

Your earthen vessels seem strong and able to run this race.

My race I must run, so He sent me to you, to gain the stamina I need to go through.

The food you feed me, highly seasoned with love, is a great testimony for our Father above.

My spiritual training from elementary to now, is a masters' degree towards my golden crown.

From higher heights, to deeper depths, with you as my Pastors, I will get there yet.

When I enter through that open door, all praises and honor to whom I adore.

To God whom is first in my life, then to my beloved Pastor and his beloved wife.

I thank you for the time invested in me and showing me a life beyond what I can see.

Father God, thank you for Pastors after your own heart, for the perfecting of the saints, which I am now a part!

An Ode to a Prophetic Song-Stress

To hear in the prophetic, oh what a wonderful thing, to listen and understand then lift your voice and sing.

Sing to the glory of God, in worship and in praise. The Lord wishes to honor you and lengthen your days.

O sing unto the Lord a new song and exalt him all day long…you are the apple of His eye. You are the apple of His eye. You are the apple of His eye!

Your soothing melodies touch His heart and from His presence, you will never part.

A pure love, a love that is true for the talent that is within you. When God was creating, He only knew what a void this earth would have without the presence of you.

God wants you to continue to hear and never fear.

Your prophetic singing is heavenly music to the untamed ear.

He gave you a talent, tailor made for you and with it you know just what to do.

Always rejoice in the remembrance of His holiness and receive with open arms the manner in which you are blessed!

Everything

God knows everything that happens in life, He knows your misery and strife.

You can make a difference it is up to you to control what you do.

When things happen, do not think it is odd, what have you done that was not of God!

Those moments where you survived allowed growth in your character to arrive.

God knows everything, yes indeed. He is the one who will supply what you need.

Listen to God and follow His way, He orders your steps every day!

Free Indeed!

Is your life in God's order? Stop straddling the fence and standing on the border.

Take that step over the line and see if you will not be all God wants you to be.

A mighty son and worker for Him, working out your salvation and showing them.

A life for God is being free from worrying about your every need.

Each day comes with its own set of troubles, they may exist but do not flee, because he whom the Lord has made free is free indeed!

Peace

PEACE... *you want peace you say. PEACE... will it come one day?*
PEACE ... it is not that far away   PEACE!

PEACE ... it is in the hearts and minds, Peace ...of every man who finds
PEACE ... Jesus the Christ his friend, Peace ... Oh what a joy to comprehend!
PEACE ...Only then will we find peace, Peace ... in the north, south, west and east
PEACE...If you seek His face and Saving Grace, you will find true peace in this human race!
PEACE ... Come rest in His Peace ...PEACE!

Relationships

My sneakers once were white and blue. I wore them often when they were new, but now
They are stain with chicken stew and the days I wear them are very few.
I once had sneakers blue and white, the style and texture were out of sight.
The left was a little bigger then the right, but they matched my feet and did not fit tight.
I wore those sneakers day and night, but between wear and tear, they lost the fight.

The beauty is gone! I will buy some more and just move on!

Alvina Y. Platt-Gregory

Reveal

I want others to see what God has done for me. Giving Him all glory as I tell this story of His presence in my life. The things He has done, doing and is going to do all because I followed and sought His advice.

The bible is the blueprint of the plans He laid out for me but there is another book covering every niche and cranny. If I get snag on the temptation hook, I can go to my father, repent and He will find the page in the book. That reveals where I should be in my life and guide me there then cover me with His tender loving care.

I Sought God

I was searching for relief from my grief, in any open arms that would embrace me.

When I look back now, on my face is a frown because I was blind and did not see

That their motives were not pure. They were using me for sure!

Without thought in my head, they lead me to bed, empty inside still unfed.

I was beating myself up, not caring or loving me.

It was not until I sought God that my aching soul was set free!

Shining Star

The life you live is not your own, do not get comfortable here because this body it is not your home!

It is a temporary vessel to help you survive in the environment that you live in,

It is keeping you alive.

Today is your birthday you are now twenty-five!

There are great things laid up for you so do not break your stride.

You ran twenty-five laps around the track of life and you did it with some help and good advice.

Enjoy life and your ordered steps, stay on the straight path and all your needs will be meant.

Go! Grow! Glow!

Let everybody know that a bright and shining star is who you really are!

Happy Birthday! This is the first day of a new season in your life!

Alvina Y. Platt-Gregory

A Radiant Light

You will have such a radiant light when you return from a God flight.

A flight of listening and receiving the word, getting information that you never heard.

Spending time with God, the creator of all, adds a cushion to your account to buffer a fall.

We are not perfect but we should try our best to push, press and pass our test.

What a radiant light shining from our face, when we do nothing to cause our God disgrace.

When we run with patience and endurance at a steady pace, overtaking procrastination to come in first place.

Let your radiant light shine!

The Stone

I can hear the ka-plop of the stone as it separates the water to claim its rightful place at the bottom of the lake.

I can see the drops of water taking flight in celebration of his arrival.
The stone is not alone, on the bottom he found many new friends.

"Shoes, The Different Souls of Man"*

When you are walking in life, through misery and strife, through joy and pain...
Does your soul exclaim!
I know Jesus. I am a son of God!
In such a crowd, what are the odds?
(*inspired by the art work of Diana Riukas)*

Alvina Y. Platt-Gregory

Thank You

FOR...

The uniqueness and style you wear in your smile.

For your strength and what you represent!

Things Happen

Everything in life is order by God, when things happen do not think it is odd.

It is for your character building, a for-shadow of things to be. These are order steps from the father to make a better you and me.

I Am

I am who I am, a vessel of the Lord, sent with a purpose from the one I adore.

In whatever I do, in whatever I say, the Will of God must have its way.

In His essences and nature I can proclaim, I am a god walking in Jesus' name!

The Great Sacrifice

The resurrection was the correction that only Jesus could make.

All the things man did, He had to die. It was no mistake.

To sacrifice himself, stretched out on a cross, full body exposed except for a loincloth.

The chastisement of my peace was upon Him that day and by His stripes, I am healed and Free to walk away.

The sweat running down His brow was intermingled with blood.

The sky was darker then the day of the flood.

The pain from the nails in His hands and in His feet, won the victory in the battle against Depression and defeat.

"My God, My God", He wailed in a weak voice. To pay for redemption of souls was my choice!

I love you to life, so live for me and stand strong in the storm like the great oak tree.

To Thine Own Self Be True

I cried when my mother died:

Miss Lillie Bell, Miss Lillie Bell, what am I to do?
Now that you are gone beyond the sky of blue.
I watched you as you lived and to thine own self you were true,
Miss Lillie Bell, Miss Lillie Bell, what am I to do?

She answered:
Live as you were taught … live as you ought.
Walk the walk and talk the talk, to thine own self be true.
Love your neighbor as yourself … treat everybody right…
Remember I will be watching you, even though I am out of sight!

God knows your every move and now I know them too.
Be not deceived to thine own self be true!

Can't Stay

The time has come for me to move on.

The place called the homestead, to me is now dead.

No more laughter or joy from the days of old, only conflict and confusion to hear the story told.

The laughing spirit that lived in these walls, now only dwell within me.

Even the house wants me to move and be free!

Free of the family and their agony.

To do it their way, why do you want to stay?

A new home is waiting for you with warm hearty neighbors on a tree line street,

The peace and tranquility just cannot be beat!

Move on! Move as soon as you can but before you do, put it in the Master's hand.

Guide me oh Lord, I pray this day, lead me to my new home because here I cannot stay.

Alvina Y. Platt-Gregory

True Freedom

When my burdens are light, I can take a flight and soar like the eagles or ride the wind like a kite.

I can run and not faint, be a soldier and a saint because the joy of the Lord is my strength.

True freedom rings when I can do all things through Christ whom I represent!

You

You are a complete sentence!

A complete sentence has words necessary for a clear expression of an essential idea.

It must be capable of standing alone and making sense.

YOU have a subject... your God given purpose.

YOU are a verb ... a person of action.

YOU are a comma ... you take a pause for the cause to meet the need.

YOU are a preposition ...connecting the unconnected.

YOU are a period ... you stand on the word and that is your final answer!

To summarize, YOU are a sentence with a purpose of action, helping others connect to the power of Life!

Twenty-Five

I am twenty-five and don't take no jive, I know where I am going in life or do I?

I have only just begun to live and have fun, I am moving at such a pace I have to run.

I can work all day then come home and play, I remember to stop and smell the roses along the way!

I am not hurting anyone, there is no one to betray so let me live and enjoy,

All I can while I am employed.

I don't ask anyone for a single red cent!

When I am old, I can smile as I look back on my style and declare it was time well spent!

The Nifty Fifties

The nifty fifties is the title given to this age. It is a milestone, an experienced monitoring gage.

Fond memories from the days of old, filled with exciting stories to be told,

Such a valuable age, it is associated with gold.

Yes, the nifty fifties is an age to behold!

It is exciting turning fifty, you have only just begun with all the wisdom and knowledge you gained, you deserve to have fun!

The spotlight is on you. Please take the middle stage.

You have earned it. You have come halfway through a century engaged...

In all kinds of activities sharing your talents and skills.

Turning fifty is not over the HILL!

Enjoy this day and have it your way, listen with both ears to what I have to say.

Learn from me for this is not the end, I am going around to see another fifty again!

Walk Away

Jesus took on our sins so we do not have to wear them. He bored them so we do not have to hoard them.

Jesus released me from my penalty, no longer blind I now can see, He did it all just for me!

The Wrath of God departed from man when Jesus intervened and made a stand.

He took it all to Calvary and purposed in His heart to make me free.

Be free and walk away from sin, Jesus died for us once and will not do it again!

Unconditional Love

There is an unconditional love that comes from heaven above, a love so pure, compassionate and sweet.

To receive this love from God above there are no requirements you have to meet.

Am I included in this love and worthy of such a treat?

Yes, even me can receive His love and walk beyond the shadow of defeat!

Whenner

When I am humble and meek, the Lord will guide my feet,

When I trust and obey, He can have His way,

When I seek His face, everything falls in place!

When I run with patience in this race, I will never wear the garment of disgrace.

When through me God proves His perfect Will, I rest in the battle if I just keep still.

God is love and full of wonder, I will not cross His Will to feel the thunder of His terrible swift sword!

When I seek His face and not His hand and do the Will I do not understand,

My God is awesome and has a plan that includes every woman, child and man.

I am a whenner, therefore I WIN!

Alvina Y. Platt-Gregory

Dr. Martin Luther King Jr.

Who was the junior of Martin Luther King?
He was the man that shouted, "Let freedom ring".
He was the man who was color-blind and never did see the color line.
He helped man gain some of his equal rights.
He organized many of non-violent fights.

His speeches were the hammer hitting the head of the nail,
The truth he spoke upset others so they put him in jail.
Not only once did he fall as prey, to silent him was their only way.
They fast-forwarded their plan to stop the man and put his program on pause,
We must play his dream shout and scream then stand strong for his cause!
Shout it over again until we see each other as a brother and a friend.

In a Season

As the seasons come and go so must I, but go where?

To higher ground and taste the new things that are all around.

Better things to help me grow, other things I need to know.

I am getting out of the box now that the lid has been removed,

I am not going to miss my chance of getting out of this groove.

Comfortability is fine for a while, but change is inevitable so give your life a new style!

Modern tech, what the heck!

I cannot resist it any longer. Keeping accurate in this field will help my confidence grow stronger.

"I know what to do", "I can do that too", these spoken words bring new life to the soul,

I still have it, my mind is sharp, I am productive and not old!

Thank you Lord!

My season has changed. My new order steps have my life rearranged.

Life is beautiful when you live for Him.

Walk in your order steps and avoid acting on a whim.

BE ORGANIZED…GET GOD-ANIZED!

Alvina Y. Platt-Gregory

Steps To Developing A Spirit Of Persistence

1. Set a goal that demands your best.
2. Develop a burning desire to make it a reality.
3. Keep your eyes on the goal.
4. Refuse to listen to negative criticism.
5. Surround yourself with encouraging friends.
6. In every defeat, look for a personal lesson.
7. Practice self-control. Do not let your emotions control you.
8. Stay in the word of God and do not give into your feelings.
9. Believe you can reach your goal because God will not give you more than you can bare.
10. Rely upon God to enable and strengthen you…Do Not Quit!

God is more persistence then you, he will never give up on you so do not give up on yourself. After you are fully persuade you shall receive the promise. Rekindle your goals and steps in the direction God has for you.

Part 2

Let us Pray … uplifting prayers that will tickle God's ear.

Praying each day before starting on your way will make your pathway clear.
You can walk without fear knowing that the angels will always be near,
Waiting to serve your spoken word.
Starting your day another way is absurd!

All prayers contain scriptures from the King James Bible.
Make a prayer list and reflect on it daily.

A Prayer for Our Governments

Hallelujah, we thank you Lord for inviting us to come and reason together. Though our sins are as scarlet, they shall be as white as snow. Thank you, Father God. We come before you to pray for a spirit of integrity in our city, state and federal government. We make ourselves subject unto the higher powers ordain by God. Psalms 1 says bless is the man that walketh not in the council of the ungodly nor sitteth in the seat of the scornful nor standeth in the way of sinners, for his delight is in the law of the Lord, which he doth meditate day and night. Let them obey your law, the Divine Law! Let the earthly higher powers bow and serve the heavenly higher power!

In Jesus' name, Amen!

A Prayer of Praise and Thanksgiving

Hallelujah is the highest praise. We thank you Lord for lending an ear to our petition. We thank you Lord for waiting to perform your word for your name' sake. I pray for things that be not as they should. There is power in speaking your word and we thank you for listening.

Thank you for directing and guiding us with your minds' eye. With thanksgiving in our hearts, we praise you! Hallelujah, AMEN.

A Prayer to Become Trusted Prayer Warriors

Father God, we pray to become trusted prayer warriors on behalf of our city, the lost and all that concerns us. Father, hear our prayer because prayer is powerful! You did not give us a spirit of fear but of power, love and a sound mind. The strong shall bear the infirmities of the weak and we cast all our cares on you because you care for us. Father, teach us to walk like Jesus daily and go forth and prove what is that good, acceptable and perfect will of God.

We ask that you mold us into trusted prayer warriors for you are the potter and we are the clay. We pray this in Jesus name, AMEN!

A Prayer to Break Strongholds

Almighty God, we thank you for the unity of prayer and fasting in order that the strongholds of Satan are broken in our lives, our city and our nation. We thank you for your word. Your word is a powerful weapon that pulls down the strongholds of the devil/our enemy. We pray against (name the strongholds you want God to tear down) In Jesus name we pray, AMEN!

A Prayer To Receive Holiness

Father God, it is in the name of Jesus that we come before you today ready to receive your Holiness. You said in your word to be holy because you are holy. We are ready to be doers of your word and not hearers only. We want a lifestyle change. We no longer want to conform to this world but we want to be transform by the renewing of our minds. We need your strength to become partakers of your holiness. We ask this in Jesus name, AMEN!

A Prayer for Sanctification

My prayer is that the very God of peace sanctify me and that my spirit, body and soul will be receive as blameless until the coming of our Lord Jesus Christ. I give you a YES and come before you with a broken and contrite heart asking you to accept me back into your fold.

In Jesus name, I pray, AMEN!

An Opening Prayer

Good morning Almighty God, our creator, provider, protector and our guide.

Thank you for ordering our steps this day. We bless the name of Jesus and forget not all our benefits. We come before you with thanksgiving in our hearts and ask that you look on our love ones and heal our weaken vessels. All power is in your hands and by your stripes we are healed. Thank you for breathing the breath of life in us and allowing us to be a part of your world one more time. In Jesus name, we pray, AMEN!